A CHRISTIAN ACTIVITY BOOKLET

Coretta Wren

Detroit, MI USA

Know ME! A Christian Activity Booklet
2nd Edition

© 2006 Coretta Wren

All rights reserved. No part of this publication may be reproduced, stored in a retrieval system, or transmitted in any form or by any means – electronic, mechanical, photocopy, recording, or any other – except for brief quotations in printed reviews, without the prior permission of the publisher.

Know Me! Publications
URL: http://www.knowmepubulication.com

in association with

PriorityONE Publications
P. O. Box 361332
Grosse Pointe, MI 48236
313-312-5318
URL: http://www.priorityonebooks.com
E-mail: info@priorityonebooks.com

ISBN 10: 1-933972-01-7
ISBN 13: 978-1-933972-01-5

Cover and interior design by PriorityONE Publications

Printed in the United States of America

Dedication

I would thank my grandparents and parents for instilling in me the foundation of the word of God and teaching true morality and humility.

A thank you goes out to all the people that have come into my life and imparted a piece of wisdom that has brought me to a point of true understanding. Your words of wisdom and caring have helped to bring me to this point of maturity.

Coretta Wren

Endorsement

"Coretta has produced a wonderfully productive and entertaining tool that provides children and adults with fun activities that test and teach our biblical knowledge and understanding."

Thank you for sharing your gift with us!"

Bishop William H. Murphy, Jr.
New Mt. Moriah Missionary Baptist Church
Senior Pastor

Seek and Find:

DIRECTIONS:
Find the words hidden in this word.
See how many you can find!

What number book is this?

LAMENTATIONS

1. _____
2. _____
3. _____
4. _____
5. _____
6. _____
7. _____
8. _____
9. _____
10. _____
11. _____
12. _____
13. _____
14. _____
15. _____
16. _____
17. _____
18. _____
19. _____
20. _____

The Body

Each of these titles are apart of the body. Place them in their proper place. Draw an arrow to the part of the body the name represents.

Pastor
Teacher
Choir
Deacon
Evangelism
Missionary
Members

Security
Ushers
Musicians
Trustees
Ministers
Outreach

Place these titles in their proper place on the body.

Scripture Memory

Can you identify where the Scripture is?

DIRECTIONS:
Write the book, chapter, and verse of the passage of scripture.

1. The Lord is my shepherd _____

2. Hallowed by thy name _____

3. Let there be light _____

4. Will a man rob God? _____

5. In the beginning was the word _____

6. Blessed is the man _____

7. For God so loved the world _____

8. He maketh me to lie down in green pastures _____

9. Blessed are the peace makers _____

10. He maketh me to lie down _____

Match Scripture

DIRECTIONS:
Draw a line from the scripture reference to the verse.

I indeed baptize
you with water.

I drew them.

b. Matthew 6:11

d. John 1:1

a. Matthew 3:11

e. Hosea 11:4

c. Isaiah 9:10

Take counsel together and it shall come to naught: speak the word and it shall not stand: for God is with you.

The bricks have fallen down, but we will rebuild with dressed stone;

In the beginning was the word.

What am I?

DIRECTIONS:
Circle all the words relating to this picture and place the answer to the above question on the line below.

```
              holy
        Lord      dance
         worship    praise
      glorify  laughter   against     gathering place   blessing
   ┌─────────────────────────────┐    building          glorify
   │ connection  repent  business│    holy              ministry
   │ free         place   apart  │    hands             fellowship
   │    pastor           hate  one│   praises           praise
   │ oneness   deacon   faulty   │    free              worship
   │    outgoing         many    │    cherish           servant
   │ fellowship  cherish  ministry│   oneness           purify
   │    loving         building  │    apart             connection
   │ welcome                     │    follow            repent
   └─────────────────────────────┘
```

_____

Can You Guess?

DIRECTIONS:
Can you guess what the word is from the clues? Place it on the line below. Then color the picture.

serpent

slaying

knowledge

first son

fruit

_____

Seek and Find:

DIRECTIONS:
Find the words hidden in this word.
See how many you can find!

What number book is this?

REVELATIONS

1. _____
2. _____
3. _____
4. _____
5. _____
6. _____
7. _____
8. _____
9. _____
10. _____

11. _____
12. _____
13. _____
14. _____
15. _____
16. _____
17. _____
18. _____
19. _____
20. _____

Find the Promised Land

DIRECTIONS:
You are an Israelite trying to get to the Promised Land. Can you get out of the wilderness?

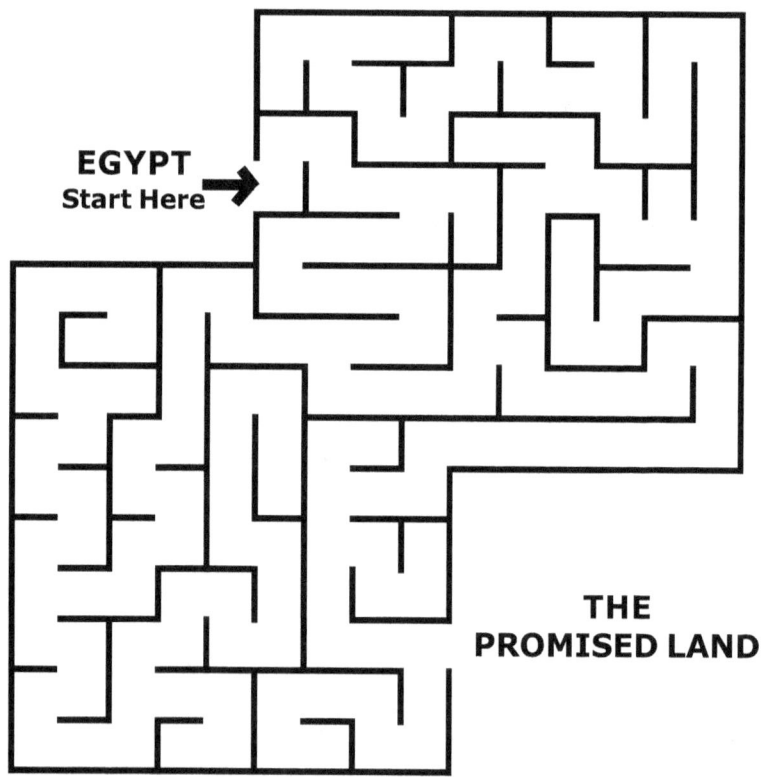

Where Do I Go?

DIRECTIONS:
1. Place these books of the Bible in alphabetical order.
2. Place these books of the Bible in order as they appear in the Bible.

1. SAMUEL
2. PROVERBS
3. GENESIS
4. NUMBERS
5. MATTHEW
6. HEBREWS
7. PSALMS
8. LUKE
9. TIMOTHY
10. MICAH
11. TITUS
12. I KINGS
13. AMOS
14. HAGGAI

Unscramble

DIRECTIONS:
Unscramble the letters above to form words and names found in the Bible.

1. SJESU _____

2. LVATISANO _____

3. OCSRS _____

4. VELO _____

5. EUSAML _____

6. EJUD _____

7. CIMHA _____

8. SJUOHA _____

9. DGUEJS _____

10. VILRANETOSE _____

11. BSPEVBOR _____

12. COJBA _____

Hidden Words

DIRECTIONS:
Find the hidden words. Words may be forward, backward, up, down, or diagonal.

J	M	A	H	A	R	B	A	J
O	A	N	G	E	L	O	S	O
S	I	C	O	L	I	D	K	H
E	N	G	O	X	V	Y	E	N
P	A	C	E	B	E	R	I	O
H	I	S	I	N	D	C	M	S
S	M	E	Y	E	A	L	E	B
W	A	S	A	D	T	O	L	H
E	R	O	E	L	L	O	E	E
N	Y	M	O	A	O	K	U	N
O	U	E	I	D	U	E	M	D

WORD LIST

ABRAHAM	SON
JOSEPH	MOSES
JOHN	YEA
SIN	BODY
BLOOD	LIVE
ASK	MARY
ANGEL	

Color Me

Cities of the Bible

DIRECTIONS:
Find the names of cities in the bible listed below. Names may be forward, backward, up, down, or diagonal.

J	E	R	U	S	A	L	E	M	M
U	N	O	D	I	Z	A	C	R	S
D	D	M	D	T	G	I	B	E	A
A	C	E	E	P	H	E	S	U	S
H	T	U	J	Y	K	F	P	V	S
J	A	H	E	G	F	A	S	S	S
A	E	T	E	E	C	E	E	R	G
D	D	V	R	N	R	A	M	A	H
C	A	N	A	A	N	F	R	H	F
B	E	T	H	L	E	H	E	M	X

CITY LIST

Jerusalem
Capua
Greece
Judah
Bethlehem
Ramah

Rome
Egypt
Ephesus
Canaan
Zidon

Women in the Bible

DIRECTIONS:
Find the names of the women in the bible listed below. Names may be forward, backward, up, down, or diagonal. There are three names not in this word search. Circle them on the list.

B	I	L	A	H	Y	L	O	M	A	N
L	O	X	D	I	E	R	C	E	A	A
O	E	E	A	A	E	O	A	R	O	R
T	H	V	H	B	O	Z	A	G	R	A
A	A	O	E	H	H	N	Y	D	A	T
N	R	K	T	I	M	A	N	E	C	H
T	A	X	H	A	L	I	Z	X	H	A
H	S	T	B	I	L	H	A	H	E	Z
L	U	D	E	B	O	R	A	H	L	K
R	A	O	M	A	R	Y	I	E	O	L

NAME LIST

Ruth	Rebekah
Martha	Rachel
Mary	Bilhah
Naomi	Leah
Sarah	Dinah
Eve	Deborah
Adah	Hagar
Zilah	Timan

Children in the Bible

DIRECTIONS:
Find the names of generations of children in the bible listed below. Names may be forward, backward, up, down, or diagonal.

B	G	E	R	S	H	K	S	I	U	Z
O	A	R	H	G	K	O	H	I	Y	E
C	I	A	R	A	N	H	O	L	X	O
A	R	C	L	I	S	A	B	A	N	L
J	A	H	T	H	I	T	A	T	O	N
O	R	E	O	R	A	H	L	H	H	E
S	E	L	A	X	E	N	P	P	S	B
E	M	R	G	O	N	I	A	A	R	U
P	E	L	O	T	A	N	E	N	E	E
H	A	S	E	N	A	T	H	Q	G	R

NAME LIST

Baalhanan
Jacob
Uz
Aran
Lotan
Shobal
Gershon
Kohath

Rachel
Asenath
Naphtali
Goni
Er
Reuben
Joseph
Merari

Men in the Bible

DIRECTIONS:
Find the names of men in the bible listed below. Names may be forward, backward, up, down, or diagonal.

H	A	V	I	D	E	Z	E	K	I	E	L
A	M	S	U	S	E	J	O	E	L	A	X
I	O	A	D	E	Y	E	T	E	H	T	O
N	S	E	A	O	T	H	O	Y	O	L	H
A	I	S	V	T	A	U	A	E	L	E	A
H	X	O	I	I	Y	M	T	E	L	T	I
P	E	H	D	K	O	A	I	I	A	A	A
E	S	A	E	Y	L	N	S	L	C	L	C
Z	B	Z	E	I	A	H	O	L	I	I	I
O	E	O	P	D	A	U	H	S	O	J	M

NAME LIST

David
Pilate
Jesus
Joshua
Ezekiel
Joel
Jehu
Ahyam

Micaiah
Zephaniah
Daniel
Amos
Hosea
Obadiah
Elisha

The Names of God

DIRECTIONS:
Find the names of the names of God in the bible listed below. Names may be forward, backward, up, down, or diagonal.

E	L	Y	E	H	W	E	H	S	H	A	L	O	M	S	Y	A	Y
L	E	D	N	O	Y	L	E	L	E	D	X	Q	I	V	A	L	A
O	A	L	D	S	S	D	O	R	L	V	S	R	M	R	H	M	H
H	R	R	S	A	Z	R	G	E	O	I	D	W	O	H	W	I	W
I	S	I	C	H	D	S	R	S	L	A	D	X	Y	E	E	G	E
M	I	Y	V	L	A	O	T	Z	A	D	V	R	Q	A	H	H	H
V	Y	H	B	G	O	D	N	T	M	D	A	Y	I	K	Y	T	S
C	H	R	M	U	F	E	T	A	O	A	O	N	T	I	I	Y	H
S	S	W	K	K	Y	I	Y	B	I	H	V	N	T	O	R	K	A
H	O	H	H	Y	Q	F	R	D	W	S	N	C	A	R	E	G	M
E	D	A	G	I	S	D	V	C	R	L	Y	U	W	L	H	D	M
W	E	Y	M	H	G	C	F	V	F	E	E	H	I	E	C	R	A
H	Q	O	Y	A	H	W	E	H	N	I	S	S	I	N	D	O	H
A	Y	A	H	W	E	H	T	S	I	D	K	E	N	U	O	L	E
Y	A	H	W	E	H	E	L	O	H	E	Y	I	S	R	A	E	L

NAME LIST

Elohim
El Elyon
El Shaddai
Yahweh Nissi
Yahweh Elohe Yisrael
Yehweh Shalom
Yahweh Tsidkenu
Attiq Yomi

Yahweh
El Roi
Yahweh-Yireh
Adonai
Qedosh Yisrael
El Olam
Yahweh Shammah

What Do They Mean?

DIRECTIONS:
Below are different names of God. Write down what each one means.

1. Elohim _____

2. Yahweh _____

3. El Elyon _____

4. El Roi _____

5. El Shaddai _____

6. Yahweh-Yireh _____

7. Yahweh Nissi _____

8. Adonai _____

9. Yahweh Elohe Yisrael _____

10. Qedosh Yisrael _____

11. El Olam _____

12. Yahweh Tsidkeme _____

13. Yahweh Shammah _____

14. Attiq Yomi _____

Unscramble

DIRECTIONS:
Can you guess the word? After you unscramble the word, how many other words can you find?

HEHNEIAM

_____

1. _____
2. _____
3. _____
4. _____
5. _____
6. _____
7. _____
8. _____
9. _____
10. _____
11. _____
12. _____
13. _____
14. _____
15. _____
16. _____
17. _____
18. _____
19. _____
20. _____
21. _____
22. _____
23. _____
24. _____
25. _____
26. _____
27. _____
28. _____
29. _____
30. _____

Unscramble

DIRECTIONS:
Can you guess the word? After you unscramble the word, how many other words can you find?

TEEONMDYUOR

_____

1. _____
2. _____
3. _____
4. _____
5. _____
6. _____
7. _____
8. _____
9. _____
10. _____
11. _____
12. _____
13. _____
14. _____
15. _____
16. _____
17. _____
18. _____
19. _____
20. _____
21. _____
22. _____
23. _____
24. _____
25. _____
26. _____
27. _____
28. _____
29. _____
30. _____

COLOR ME

WHO AM I?

_____

Coding

DIRECTIONS:
Using the numbers assigned to each alphabet, decode each line to discover the hidden names. The first one has been done for you.

A	B	C	D	E	F	G	H	I
1	2	3	4	5	6	7	8	9

J	K	L	M	N	O	P	Q	R
10	11	12	13	14	15	16	17	18

S	T	U	V	W	X	Y	Z
19	20	21	22	23	24	25	26

1. __A__ __B__ __R__ __A__ __H__ __A__ __M__
     1   2   18   1   8   1   13

2. __ __ __ __ __ __ __
   18   5   2   5   11   1   8

3. __ __ __ __ __
   12   1   2   1   14

4. __ __ __ __ __
   10   1   3   15   2

5. __ __ __ __
   5   19   1   21

6. __ __ __ __
   19   5   9   18

7. __ __ __ __ __
   9   19   1   1   3

8. __ __ __ __ __ __
   18   1   3   8   5   12

9. __ __ __ __ __ __
   16   5   14   9   5   12

10. __ __ __ __ __ __ __ __ __
    16   1   4   1   14   1   18   1   14

More Coding

DIRECTIONS:
Finish decoding the remaining names on your list. Then find the 14 decoded names in the word search at the bottom of this page.

A	B	C	D	E	F	G	H	I
1	2	3	4	5	6	7	8	9

J	K	L	M	N	O	P	Q	R
10	11	12	13	14	15	16	17	18

S	T	U	V	W	X	Y	Z
19	20	21	22	23	24	25	26

11. _____ 19 21 3 3 15 20 8

12. _____ 19 8 5 3 8 1 13

13. _____ 8 11 3 15 18

14. _____ 2 5 14 15 14 9

15. _____ 13 1 13 18 5

R	P	A	S	S	P	E	N	I	E	L
O	A	H	J	B	E	N	O	N	I	S
M	O	T	A	B	R	A	H	A	M	H
A	A	O	C	O	E	C	R	I	A	E
H	N	C	O	R	B	I	A	N	M	C
E	A	C	B	K	E	K	A	R	R	H
S	R	U	C	S	K	B	O	R	E	A
A	A	S	A	R	A	C	H	E	L	M
U	M	A	N	L	H	I	S	A	A	C

Addition

DIRECTIONS:
There are 66 books in the bible. Add all the numbers. After adding them, find out which book of the bible you've added up.

1. 1+2+18+1+8+1+13 = _43_ - _JOHN_

2. 18+5+2+5+11+1+8 = _____ - _____

3. 12+1+2+1+14 = _____ - _____

4. 10+1+3+15+2 = _____ - _____

5. 5+19+1+21 = _____ - _____

6. 19+5+9+18 = _____ - _____

7. 9+19+1+1+3 = _____ - _____

8. 16+5+14+9+5+2 = _____ - _____

9. 18+1+3+8+5+12 = _____ - _____

10. 16+5+3+14+18+14 = _____ - _____

11. 19+21+6+15+20+8 = _____ - _____

12. 19+8+5+3+8+1+13 = _____ - _____

13. 8+1+13+15+18 = _____ - _____

14. 2+5+14+15+14+9 = _____ - _____

15. 13+1+13+18+5 = _____ - _____

Definitions

DIRECTIONS:
Examine the list of words below. Write 5 words that mean the same as each of the words listed.

1. Propitiation
    1. _____
    2. _____
    3. _____
    4. _____
    5. _____

2. Provocation
    1. _____
    2. _____
    3. _____
    4. _____
    5. _____

3. Predestinated
    1. _____
    2. _____
    3. _____
    4. _____
    5. _____

4. Principalities
    1. _____
    2. _____
    3. _____
    4. _____
    5. _____

5. Lordship
    1. _____
    2. _____
    3. _____
    4. _____
    5. _____

6. Longsuffering
    1. _____
    2. _____
    3. _____
    4. _____
    5. _____

More Definitions

DIRECTIONS:
Just like the previous page, examine the list of words below. Write 5 words that mean the same as each of the words listed.

7. Labor
    1. _____   4. _____
    2. _____   5. _____
    3. _____

8. Inherit
    1. _____   4. _____
    2. _____   5. _____
    3. _____

9. Interpreted
    1. _____   4. _____
    2. _____   5. _____
    3. _____

10. Justify
    1. _____   4. _____
    2. _____   5. _____
    3. _____

11. Infirmity
    1. _____   4. _____
    2. _____   5. _____
    3. _____

12. Idolater
    1. _____   4. _____
    2. _____   5. _____
    3. _____

COLOR ME
WHO AM I?

CAN YOU DRAW DANIEL IN THE LION'S DEN?

DIRECTIONS:
Read Daniel chapter 6. Try to draw Daniel in the lion's den. After you finish drawing, color it.

CAN YOU DRAW DAVID & GOLIATH?

DIRECTIONS:
Read I Samuel chapter 17. Try to draw David and Goliath. After you finish drawing, color it.

ANSWERS

Behind this page are the answers to activities within this booklet.

We decided to put them in just in case you get stumped.

But remember...

It's better when you do all you can to figure them out on your own.

In other words...
                Don't peek!

Seek and Find:
Answer Key

DIRECTIONS:
Find the words hidden in this word.
See how many you can find!

What number book is this?

LAMENTATIONS

1. men
2. late
3. son
4. sin
5. ten
6. tale
7. lame
8. meat
9. team
10. tan
11. seat
12. lent
13. ate
14. tin
15. mental
16. lament
17. Satan
18. amen
19. eat
20. tea
21. man
22. male
23. sat
24. set
25. tie
26. tent
27. teal
28. lean
29. sit
30. tale

The Body
Answer Key

Each of these titles are apart of the body. Place them in their proper place. Draw an arrow to the part of the body the name represents.

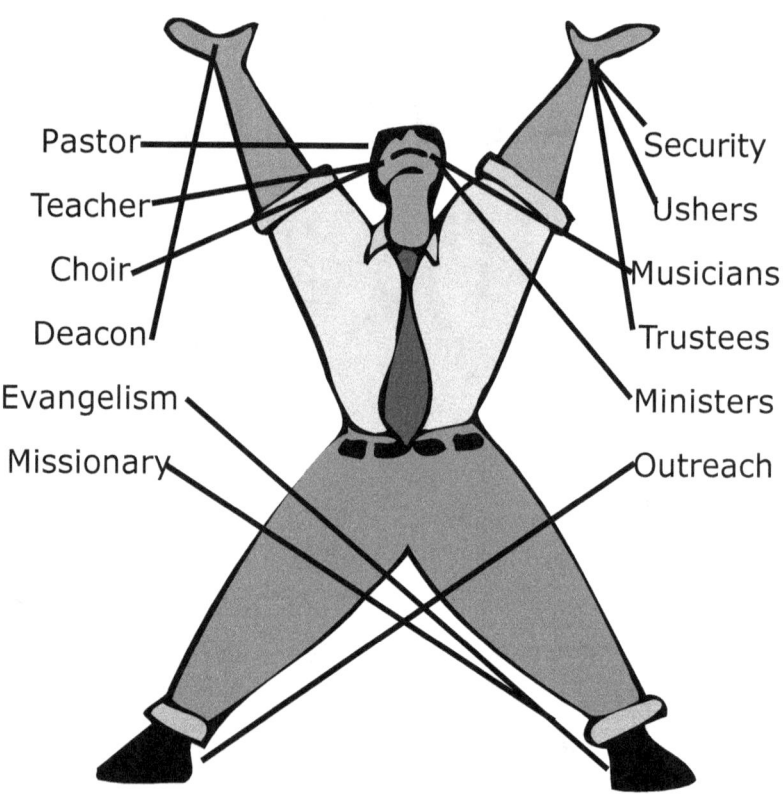

Place these titles in their proper place on the body.

Scripture Memory

Answer Key

Can you identify where the Scripture is?

DIRECTIONS:
Write the book, chapter, and verse of the passage of scripture.

1. The Lord is my shepherd _____ Psalm 23:1

2. Hallowed by thy name _____ Matthew 6:9

3. Let there be light _____ Genesis 1:3

4. Will a man rob God? _____ Malachi 3:8

5. In the beginning was the word _____ John 1:1

6. Seek ye first _____ Matthew 6:33

7. For God so loved the world _____ John 3:16

8. He maketh me to lie down in green pastures _____ Psalm 23:2

9. Blessed are the peace makers _____ Matthew 5:9

10. I am the vine _____ John 15:5

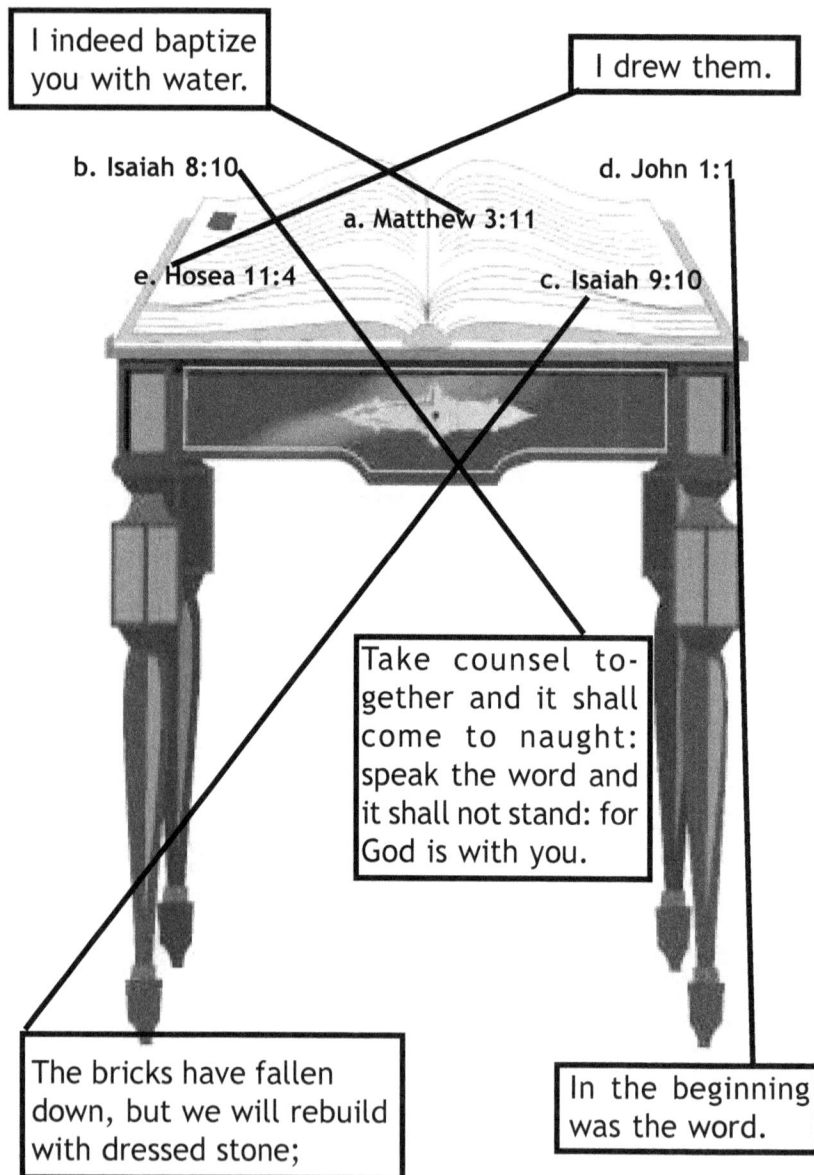

What am I?

Answer Key

DIRECTIONS:
Circle all the words relating to this picture and place the answer to the above question on the line below.

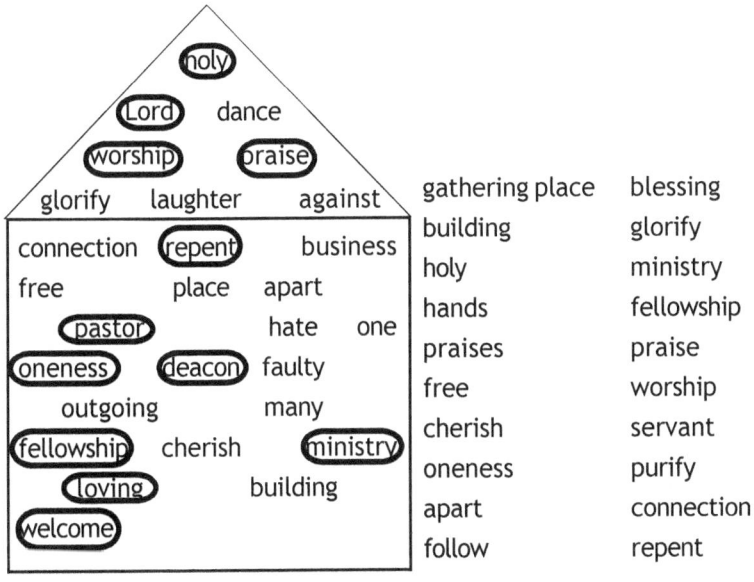

The Church
_____

Can You Guess?

DIRECTIONS:
Can you guess what the word is from the clues? Place it on the line below. Then color the picture.

serpent

slaying

knowledge

first son

fruit

TEMPTATION

_____

Seek and Find:
Answer Key

DIRECTIONS:
Find the words hidden in this word.
See how many you can find!

What number book is this?

REVELATIONS

1. reveal
2. star
3. rain
4. nations
5. late
6. tale
7. liar
8. neat
9. teen
10. rose
11. rise
12. toe
13. toes
14. store
15. elevator
16. verse
17. live
18. list
19. eat
20. tea
21. ran
22. sale
23. sat
24. set
25. tie
26. ten
27. teal
28. lean
29. sit
30. sole
31. liver
32. line
33. real
34. vote
35. lions
36. son
37. near
38. tar
39. revel
40. stare
41. tare
42. slate
43. relate
44. stair
45. relations

Find the Promised Land

Answer Key

DIRECTIONS:
You are an Israelite trying to get to the Promised Land. Can you get out of the wilderness?

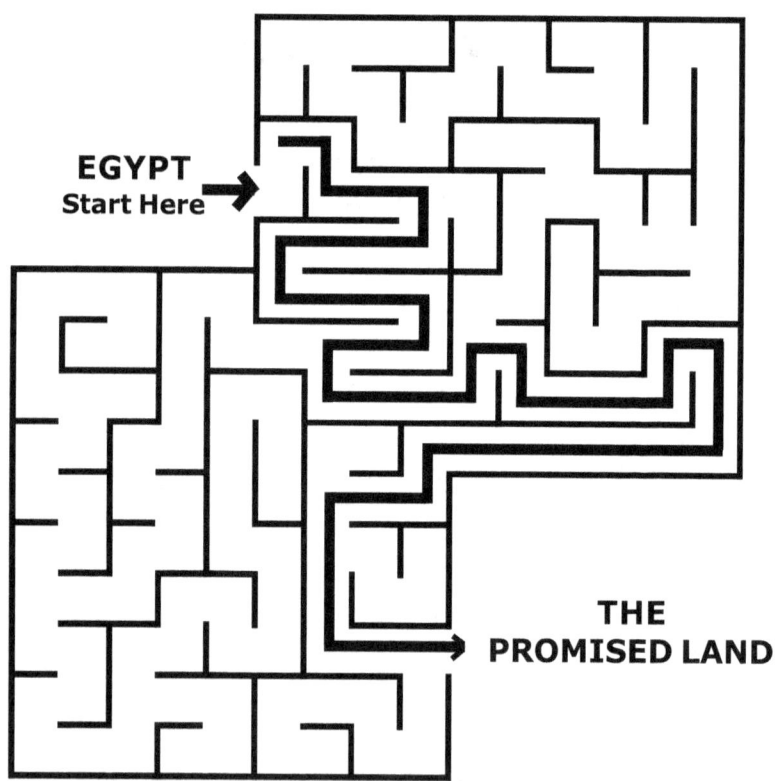

Where Do I Go?
Answer Key

DIRECTIONS:
1. Place these books of the Bible in alphabetical order.
2. Place these books of the Bible in order as they appear in the Bible.

ORIGINAL LIST	ALPHABETICAL	BIBLICAL
1. SAMUEL	1. AMOS	1. GENESIS
2. PROVERBS	2. GENESIS	2. NUMBERS
3. GENESIS	3. HAGGAI	3. SAMUEL
4. NUMBERS	4. HEBREWS	4. I KINGS
5. MATTHEW	5. LUKE	5. PSALMS
6. HEBREWS	6. I KINGS	6. PROVERBS
7. PSALMS	7. MATTHEW	7. AMOS
8. LUKE	8. MICAH	8. MICAH
9. TIMOTHY	9. NUMBERS	9. HAGGAI
10. MICAH	10. PSALMS	10. MATTHEW
11. TITUS	11. PROVERBS	11. LUKE
12. I KINGS	12. SAMUEL	12. TIMOTHY
13. AMOS	13. TIMOTHY	13. TITUS
14. HAGGAI	14 TITUS	14 HEBREWS

Unscramble
Answer Key

DIRECTIONS:
Unscramble the letters above to form words and names found in the Bible.

1. SJESU	JESUS
2. LVATISANO	SALVATION
3. OCSRS	CROSS
4. VELO	LOVE
5. EUSAML	SAMUEL
6. EJUD	JUDE
7. CIMHA	MICAH
8. SJUOHA	JOSHUA
9. DGUEJS	JUDGES
10. VILRANETOSE	REVELATIONS
11. BSPEVBOR	PROVERBS
12. COJBA	JACOB

Hidden Words
Answer Key

DIRECTIONS:
Find the hidden words. Words may be forward, backward, up, down, or diagonal.

J	M	A	H	A	R	B	A	J
O	A	N	G	E	L	O	S	O
S	I	C	O	L	I	D	K	H
E	N	G	O	X	V	Y	E	N
P	A	C	E	B	E	R	I	O
H	I	S	I	N	D	C	M	S
S	M	E	Y	E	A	L	E	B
W	A	S	A	D	T	O	L	H
E	R	O	E	L	L	O	E	E
N	Y	M	O	A	O	K	U	N
O	U	E	I	D	U	E	M	D

WORD LIST
ABRAHAM
JOSEPH
JOHN
SIN
BLOOD
ASK
ANGEL
SON
MOSES
YEA
BODY
LIVE
MARY

Cities of the Bible
Answer Key

DIRECTIONS:
Find the names of cities in the bible listed below. Names may be forward, backward, up, down, or diagonal.

J	E	R	U	S	A	L	E	M	M
U	N	O	D	I	Z	A	C	R	S
D	D	M	D	T	G	I	B	E	A
A	C	E	E	P	H	E	S	U	S
H	T	U	J	Y	K	F	P	V	S
J	A	H	E	G	F	A	S	S	S
A	E	T	E	E	C	E	E	R	G
D	D	V	R	N	R	A	M	A	H
C	A	N	A	A	N	F	R	H	F
B	E	T	H	L	E	H	E	M	X

CITY LIST

Jerusalem
Capua
Greece
Judah
Bethlehem
Ramah

Rome
Egypt
Ephesus
Canaan
Zidon

Women in the Bible
Answer Key

DIRECTIONS:
Find the names of the women in the bible listed below. Names may be forward, backward, up, down, or diagonal. There are three names not in this word search. Circle them on the list.

B	I	L	A	H	Y	L	O	M	A	N
L	O	X	D	I	E	R	C	E	A	A
O	E	E	A	A	E	O	A	R	O	R
T	H	V	H	B	O	Z	A	G	R	A
A	A	O	E	H	H	N	Y	D	A	T
N	R	K	T	I	M	A	N	E	C	H
T	A	X	H	A	L	I	Z	X	H	A
H	S	T	B	I	L	H	A	H	E	Z
L	U	D	E	B	O	R	A	H	L	K
R	A	O	M	A	R	Y	I	E	O	L

NAME LIST

Ruth
[Martha]
Mary
[Naomi]
Sarah
Eve
Adah
Zilah

Rebekah
Rachel
Bilhah
Leah
[Dinah]
Deborah
Hagar
Timan

Children in the Bible
Answer Key

DIRECTIONS:
Find the names of generations of children in the bible listed below. Names may be forward, backward, up, down, or diagonal.

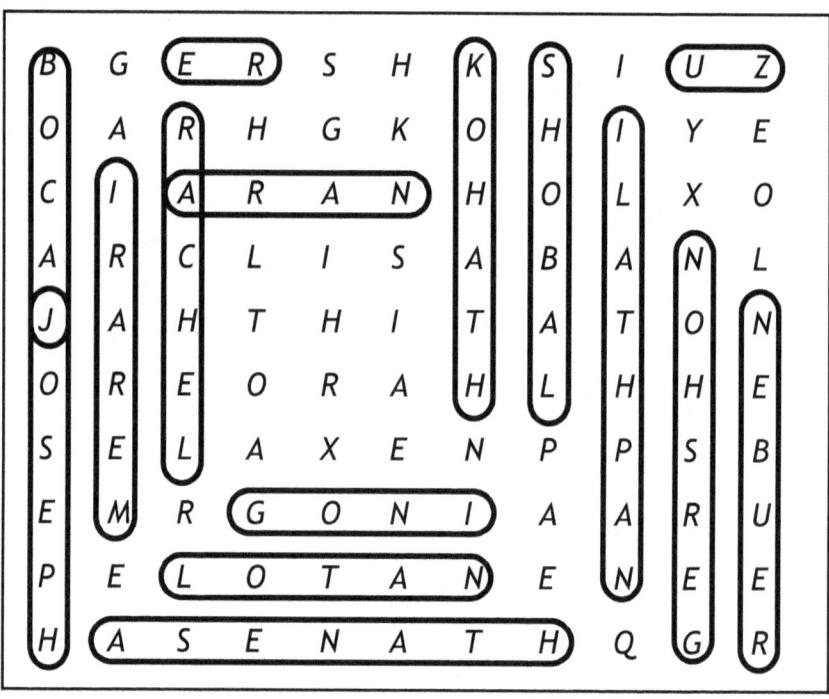

NAME LIST

Baalhanan
Jacob
Uz
Aran
Lotan
Shobal
Gershon
Kohath

Rachel
Asenath
Naphtali
Goni
Er
Reuben
Joseph
Merari

Men in the Bible
Answer Key

DIRECTIONS:
Find the names of men in the bible listed below. Names may be forward, backward, up, down, or diagonal.

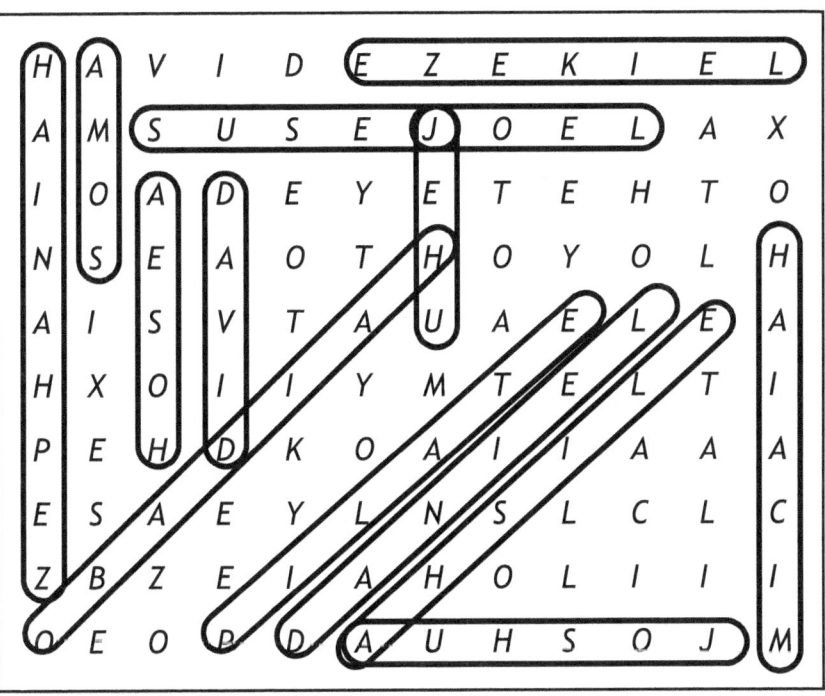

NAME LIST

David
Pilate
Jesus
Joshua
Ezekiel
Joel
Jehu
Ahyam

Micaiah
Zephaniah
Daniel
Amos
Hosea
Obadiah
Elisha

The Names of God

DIRECTIONS:
Find the names of the names of God in the bible listed below. Names may be forward, backward, up, down, or diagonal.

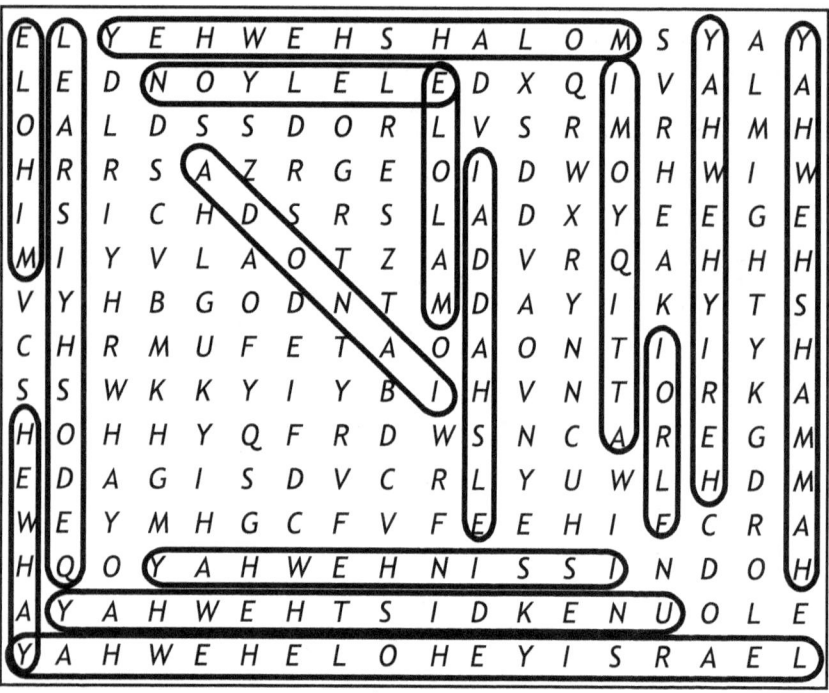

NAME LIST

Elohim
El Elyon
El Shaddai
Yahweh Nissi
Yahweh Elohe Yisrael
Yehweh Shalom
Yahweh Tsidkenu
Attiq Yomi

Yahweh
El Roi
Yahweh-Yireh
Adonai
Qedosh Yisrael
El Olam
Yahweh Shammah

What Do They Mean?
Answer Key

DIRECTIONS:
Below are different names of God. Write down what each one means.

1. Elohim — God, Judge, Creator

2. Yahweh — Lord Jehovah

3. El Elyon — The Most High God

4. El Roi — God who sees

5. El Shaddai — All Sufficient One

6. Yahweh-Yireh — The Lord will Provide

7. Yahweh Nissi — The Lord My Banner

8. Adonai — Lord, Master

9. Yahweh Elohe Yisrael — The God of Israel

10. Qedosh Yisrael — The Holy One of Israel

11. El Olam — The Everlasting God

12. Yahweh Tsidkenu — The Lord Our Righteousness

13. Yahweh Shammah — The Lord is There

14. Attiq Yomi — Ancient of Days

Unscramble

Answer Key

DIRECTIONS:
Can you guess the word? After you unscramble the word, how many other words can you find?

HEHNEIAM

_____ NEHEMIAH _____

1. reveal
2. star
3. rain
4. nations
5. late
6. tale
7. liar
8. neat
9. teen
10. rose
11. rise
12. toe
13. toes
14. store
15. elevator
16. verse
17. live
18. list
19. eat
20. tea
21. ran
22. sale
23. sat
24. set
25. tie
26. ten
27. teal
28. lean
29. sit
30. sole
31. liver
32. line
33. real
34. vote
35. lions
36. son
37. near
38. tar
39. revel
40. stare
41. tare
42. slate
43. relate
44. stair
45. relations

Unscramble
Answer Key

DIRECTIONS:
Can you guess the word? After you unscramble the word, how many other words can you find?

TEEONMDYUOR

DEUTERONOMY

1. money
2. try
3. dry
4. due
5. yet
6. not
7. toe
8. dot
9. tone
10. note
11. your
12. rode
13. door
14. tore
15. rude
16. dome
17. doom
18. moon
19. mood
20. moot
21. done
22. more
23. room
24. norm
25. true
26. root
27. moody
28. tour
29. our
30. you
31. modern
32. rue
33. rote
34. toy
35. meet
36. deem
37. tee
38. rot
39. unto
40. run
41. runt
42. nut
43. roomy
44. tree
45. tune

Decoding

Answer Key

DIRECTIONS:
Using the numbers assigned to each alphabet, decode each line to discover the hidden names. The first one has been done for you.

A	B	C	D	E	F	G	H	I
1	2	3	4	5	6	7	8	9

J	K	L	M	N	O	P	Q	R
10	11	12	13	14	15	16	17	18

S	T	U	V	W	X	Y	Z
19	20	21	22	23	24	25	26

1. A B R A H A M
   1 2 18 1 8 1 13

2. R E B E K A H
   18 5 2 5 11 1 8

3. L A B A N
   12 1 2 1 14

4. J A C O B
   10 1 3 15 2

5. E S A U
   5 19 1 21

6. S E I R
   19 5 9 18

7. I S A A C
   9 19 1 1 3

8. R A C H E L
   18 1 3 8 6 12

9. P E N I E L
   16 5 14 9 5 12

10. P A D A N A R A N
    16 1 4 1 14 1 18 1 14

More Decoding
Answer Key

DIRECTIONS:
Finish decoding the remaining names on your list. Then find the 14 decoded names in the word search at the bottom of this page.

A	B	C	D	E	F	G	H	I
1	2	3	4	5	6	7	8	9

J	K	L	M	N	O	P	Q	R
10	11	12	13	14	15	16	17	18

S	T	U	V	W	X	Y	Z
19	20	21	22	23	24	25	26

11. S U C C O T H
     19 21 3 3 15 20 8

12. S H E C H A M
     19 8 5 3 8 1 13

13. B E N O N I
     2 5 14 15 14 9

14. M A M R E
     13 1 13 18 5

R	P	A	S	S	P	E	N	I	E	L
O	A	H	J	B	E	N	O	N	I	S
M	D	T	A	B	R	A	H	A	M	H
A	A	O	C	O	E	C	R	I	A	E
H	N	C	O	R	B	I	A	N	M	C
E	A	C	B	K	E	K	A	R	R	H
S	R	U	C	S	K	B	O	R	E	A
A	A	S	A	R	A	C	H	E	L	M
U	M	A	N	L	H	I	S	A	A	C

Addition
Answer Key

DIRECTIONS:
There are 66 books in the bible. Add all the numbers. After adding them, find out which book of the bible you've added up.

1. 1+2+18+1+8+1+13   =   43   -   JOHN
2. 18+5+2+5+11+1+8   =   50   -   PHILIPPIANS
3. 12+1+2+1+14   =   30   -   AMOS
4. 10+1+3+15+2   =   31   -   OBADIAH
5. 5+19+1+21   =   46   -   I CORINTHIANS
6. 19+5+9+18   =   51   -   COLOSSIANS
7. 9+19+1+1+3   =   33   -   MICAH
8. 16+5+14+9+5+3   =   52   -   I THESSALONIANS
9. 18+1+3+8+5+12   =   47   -   II CORINTHIANS
10. 16+5+3+14+18+10   =   66   -   REVELATIONS
11. 19+21+1+15+8   =   64   -   III JOHN
12. 19+8+5+3+8+1+13   =   57   -   PHILEMON
13. 8+1+13+15+18   =   56   -   TITUS
14. 2+5+14+15+14+9   =   59   -   JAMES
15. 13+1+13+18+5   =   49   -   EPHESIANS

Definitions
Answer Key

DIRECTIONS:
Examine the list of words below. Write 5 words that mean the same as each of the words listed.

1. Propitiation
   1. appease
   2. satisfy
   3. atonement
   4. placating
   5. sacrifice

2. Provocation
   1. provoke
   2. irritate
   3. rouse
   4. bother
   5. incite

3. Predestinated
   1. Foreordain
   2. Predetermine
   3. Define
   4. Resolve
   5. Decide

4. Principalities
   1. Supreme Power
   2. Preeminent Strength
   3. Authority
   4. Force
   5. Dominion

5. Lordship
   1. Master
   2. Ruler
   3. Teacher
   4. King
   5. Commander

6. Longsuffering
   1. Patiently Enduring
   2. Long Term Suffering
   3. Endurance
   4. Inconvenient
   5. Hardship

More Definitions
Answer Key

DIRECTIONS:
Just like the previous page, examine the list of words below. Write 5 words that mean the same as each of the words listed.

7. Labor
   1. Work
   2. Task
   3. Activity
   4. Understanding
   5. Job

8. Inherit
   1. Acquire
   2. Receive
   3. Succeed
   4. Get
   5. Take Over

9. Interpreted
   1. Translate
   2. Explain
   3. Render
   4. Define
   5. Describe

10. Justly
    1. Fitting
    2. Confronting
    3. Fair
    4. Equal
    5. Righteous

11. Infirmity
    1. Weakness
    2. Debility
    3. disease
    4. Powerless
    5. Feeble

12. Idolater
    1. Worshipper
    2. Lover
    3. Zealots
    4. Admirer
    5. Adorer

References:

The answers to the activities contained in this booklet were obtained from the following Christian reference materials.

Vine's Complete Expository Dictionary of Old and New Testament Words.: Nelson Vine, Unger, White. Thomas Nelson Publisher.;

Holy Bible New Analytical Indexed Edition Dictionary and Concordance. Copyright © 1973, 1971, 1966, 1950, 1947, 1941, 1938, 1931. John A. Dickson Publishing Company. Chicago

The Word "The Bible From 26 Translations; Curtis Vaughan, Th. D. General Editor. Mathis Publishers, Inc. P. O. Box 6685; Gulfport Ms.

Holy Bible; King James Version: Words of Christ In Red Dictionary and Concordance @ 1984, 1977

ABOUT THE AUTHOR

A native Mississippian, Coretta R. Wren has been inspired to reach out by educating others about the Word of God. Coretta's inspiration comes from twenty years of educating youth as a substitute instructor. Her belief that God provides fruitful life to those who come to know Him caused her to seek an appealing method through which she could teach others and open the door to true wisdom. *"The fear of the Lord is the beginning of wisdom."*

By creatively combining fun and academic methods with biblical content Coretta is providing a tool which increases a person's knowledge of God and His Word. It can be used as an educational resource in various bible schools, youth groups, and Christian education institutions, or for those who simply like learning while they have fun.

To contact Coretta email or call:

Know Me Publications
Email: WrenKnowMePublication@Yahoo.com
Website: www.knowmepubulications.com

Book Order Form

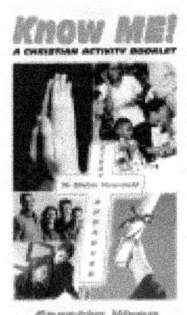

Know Me!
A Christian Activity Booklet

PLEASE PRINT CLEARLY

Name _____

Address _____

City _____ State _____ Zip _____

Phone _____ Fax _____

Email _____

Quantity	
Price *(each)*	$7.99
Subtotal	
S & H	.99
MI Tax 6%	
Total	

METHOD OF PAYMENT:

❑ Check or Money Order
(Make payable to: Coretta Wren)

❑ Visa ❑ MasterCard ❑ American Express

Acct No. _____

Expiration Date *(mmyy)* _____

Signature _____

Mail your payment to:
ATTN: Coretta Wren
PriorityONE Publications
P. O. Box 361332
Grosse Pointe, MI 48236

or call:
313-312-5318

www.ingramcontent.com/pod-product-compliance
Lightning Source LLC
Chambersburg PA
CBHW071543080526
44588CB00011B/1778